MW00768637

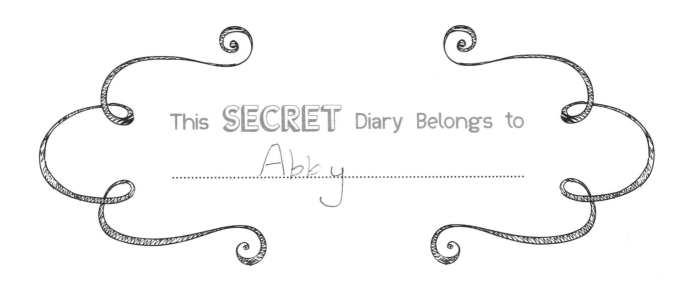

This **SECRET** Diary Belongs to

Abby

© 2014 by Barbour Publishing, Inc.

ISBN 978-1-62836-961-8

All rights reserved. No part of this publication may be reproduced or transmitted for commercial purposes, except for brief quotations in printed reviews, without written permission of the publisher.

Scripture quotations are taken from the New Life Version copyright © 1969 and 2003. Used by permission of Barbour Publishing, Inc., Uhrichsville, Ohio, 44683. All rights reserved.

Scripture quotations marked NIV are taken from the HOLY BIBLE, NEW INTERNATIONAL VERSION®. NIV®. Copyright © 1973, 1978, 1984, 2011 by Biblica, Inc.™ Used by permission. All rights reserved worldwide.

Scripture quotations marked MSG are from THE MESSAGE. Copyright © by Eugene H. Peterson 1993, 1994, 1995, 1996, 2000, 2001, 2002. Used by permission of NavPress Publishing Group.

Scripture quotations marked NLT are taken from the Holy Bible. New Living Translation copyright© 1996, 2004, 2007 by Tyndale House Foundation. Used by permission of Tyndale House Publishers, Inc. Carol Stream, Illinois 60188. All rights reserved.

Published by Barbour Publishing, Inc., P.O. Box 719, Uhrichsville, Ohio 44683, www.barbourbooks.com

Our mission is to publish and distribute inspirational products offering exceptional value and biblical encouragement to the masses.

 Member of the
Evangelical Christian
Publishers Association

Printed in China.

Shenzhen Caimei Printing Co,. Ltd, Shenzhen, China 518129; June 2014; D10004447

God ♥s me

My Secret Diary

BARBOUR
PUBLISHING

God ♥ me

"I have called you by name.
You are Mine!"
Isaiah 43:1

My full name:
Abigail

My nickname(s):
Abby

My birthday:
July 14

My hometown:

My eye color:
brown

My hair color:
black

My favorite thing about myself is...

My favorite...
color red-vilot
food spicy food
book uha was books
song or singer tayor swifft
movie
TV show
game minecraft
animal wild dog

I would describe my personality as (check all that apply)

- ☑ silly
- ☑ serious
- ☐ bubbly
- ☐ sarcastic
- ☑ smart
- ☑ shy
- ☐ outgoing
- ☑ fashionable

- ☑ graceful
- ☐ klutzy
- ☑ artistic
- ☑ musical
- ☑ athletic
- ☑ kind
- ☐ dependable
- ☐ self-confident

- ☐ sassy
- ☑ cute
- ☑ weird
- ☐ mysterious
- ☐ diva-licious
- ☐ ....
- ☐ ....
- ☐ ....

More about Me!

Thumbs up or thumbs down:

- ☑ ☑ Boys
- ☑ ☐ Gym Class
- ☑ ☐ Art/Music Class
- ☐ ☑ Makeup
- ☑ ☑ Brother(s)
- ☐ ☐ Sister(s)
- ☐ ☑ Romantic Comedies
- ☐ ☑ Fashion Mags
- ☐ ☑ Passing Notes in Class
- ☑ ☑ Nail Polish

Which one? (circle one)

Pen *or* Pencil

Talking *or* Texting

Backpack *or* Purse

Lunch Box *or* Cafeteria Tray

Singing *or* Dancing

Homework *or* Chores

Inside *or* Outside

Pool *or* Beach

Pants *or* Skirt

Flip-flops *or* Sneakers

If they made a movie about my life and adventures...

I would fant.

Here's who would play me: ....

Here's who would play my best friend: ....

Supporting characters:

....

....

....

Movie plot:

....

....

Top Secret! Shh! Top Secret!

Today in DC we helped my eemoo move in it was hard but fun because we went to the Zoo and saw the new baby panda bei bei and we saw beibei's family it was fun after that we got the most cuteis stuffed panda ever.

You made all the delicate, inner parts of my body and knit me together in my mother's womb.
Psalm 139:13 NLT

My other close friends: ....

I laugh the hardest when I remember the time we... ....

....

I knew we were true friends when... ....

....

Gal Pals Hall of Fame!

Best listener:

....

Best encourager:

....

Best dancer:

....

Best storyteller:

....

Most likely to do a cartwheel:

....

Most likely to star in a play:

....

Most likely to have a cool job:

....

Most likely to save the world:

....

"Even the very hairs of your head are all numbered."
Matthew 10:30 NIV

Doodles Doodles Doodles

My Family

I have a zany family full of special people! Here's what I love about them:

....

My parents show me they love me in many different ways. Here's my favorite way:

....

My grandparents are great, too. Here are some special memories I have about them:

....

My siblings sometimes drive me nutty, but deep down I love them! Here's why:

....

When we get together as a big group, it's a tradition that we always…

....

....

....

Adventures Fun Excitement

....

....

....

....

....

....

....

....

....

....

....

"When you call on me, when you come and pray to me, I'll listen."

Jeremiah 29:12 MSG

....

....

....

....

....

....

....

....

....

....

....

....

....

Doodle pages

And my God will give you everything you need because of His great riches in Jesus Christ.
Philippians 4:19 MSG

Fabulous Fashion Diva

....

....

....

....

....

....

....

....

....

....

....

My Fun

My favorite thing to do on a weeknight:

....

....

My favorite thing to do on a weekend:

....

....

Here's a list of the people I most like to have fun with:

....

....

....

The time I had the most fun ever was...

....

....

....

If I could plan a day of fun, it would be sure to include...

....

....

....

Here are the words I'd use to describe my idea of fun (check all that apply):

- ☑ Loud
- ☑ Colorful
- ☐ Peaceful
- ☐ Tidy
- ☑ Messy
- ☐ Crowded
- ☐ Thrilling
- ☐ Musical

- ☐ Sleepless
- ☑ Crazy
- ☐ Active
- ☐ Elegant
- ☐ Beautiful
- ☐ Busy
- ☐ ....
- ☐ ....

Know then that the Lord your God is God, the faithful God.
He keeps His promise and shows His loving-kindness to those who love Him.
Deuteronomy 7:9 NIV

My Faith

You can trust God right now to supply all your needs for today. And if your needs are bigger tomorrow, His supply will be bigger also.

Always give thanks for all things to God the Father in the name of our Lord Jesus Christ.

EPHESIANS 5:20

My blessings are too many to count! Here is a list of just a few of the things I am thankful for:

....

....

....

....

....

....

....

....

What I believe:

Your heart should be holy and set apart for the Lord God. Always be ready to tell everyone who asks you why you believe as you do. 1 PETER 3:15

When times are hard, here's what I put my hope and trust in:

....
....
....
....
....
....

Here's the truth: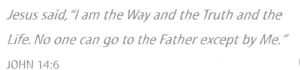

Jesus said, "I am the Way and the Truth and the Life. No one can go to the Father except by Me." JOHN 14:6

My favorite Bible verses:

....
....
....
....
....
....
....

....

....

....

....

....

....

....

....

....

....

....

....

....

....

....

LOL Memories Laughs Fun Times

"And my spirit rejoices in God my Savior."
Luke 1:47 MSG

Doodle pages

Shh! For My Eyes Only! Shh!

I'm getting a pottle soon!!! ☺

My Dreams and Goals

When I grow up, I want to be...

....
....
....
....
....
....
....
....
....
....

It's important to me that my job includes

☐ working with kids

☐ making a difference

☐ getting paid lots of money

☐ being famous

☐ being creative

☐ working with numbers

☐ working with my hands

☐ meeting new people

☐ being by myself

☐ ....

☐ ....

My secret dream job that nobody would guess is...

....

....

If I could travel anywhere, I would go to...

....

....

I know I'm the best at...

....

....

In the next year I want to...

....

....

I can't wait until I'm old enough to...

....

....

"For I know the plans I have for you," says the Lord, "plans for well-being and not for trouble, to give you a future and a hope."
JEREMIAH 29:11

To accomplish great things, we must dream as well as act.
ANATOLE FRANCE

Shoot for the moon. Even if you miss, you'll land among the stars.
LES BROWN

*Our hope comes from God. May He fill you
with joy and peace because of your trust in Him*
Romans 15:13

....

....

....

....

....

....

....

....

....

....

....

....

Sweet Sassy Cute Fun Silly

My Favorite Hang-Outs

My bedroom is the place where I like to. . .

....

....

If I could have a bedroom makeover, here's what I would include:

....

....

My friends and I have the most fun when spending time at. . .

....

....

....

The best place to hang out if we want some privacy is...

....

....

....

....

My favorite wintertime hang-out:

....

....

....

....

My favorite summertime hang-out:

....

....

....

....

I can do all things because Christ gives me strength.
Philippians 4:13

Gal Pals Peeps Girls BFFs

....

....

....

....

....

....

....

....

....

Doodles Doodles Doodles

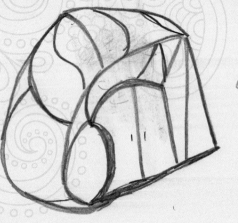

a crabs
shell, !
get it !

HaHa Ha Ha

"For I know the plans I have for you," declares the LORD, "plans to prosper you and not to harm you, plans to give you hope and a future."
Jeremiah 29:11 NIV

....

....

....

....

....

....

....

....

....

....

....

My School

My school's name:

....

Our mascot:

....

My school is best known for:

....

....

....

....

....

I describe school as

☐ cool

☐ fun

☐ challenging

☐ difficult

☐ interesting

☐ confusing

☐ exciting

☐ boring

☐ ....

☐ ....

☐

Class

My favorite subject:

....

My least favorite subject:

....

My favorite teacher:

....

The teacher who gives the most homework:

....

....

Lunch

Who sits at my lunch table:

....

My favorite menu item:

....

My favorite dessert/snack:

....

After we're done eating, we usually spend the rest of the lunch period..

....

Class superlatives

Most likely to start a fashion trend:

....

Best hair color:

....

Best laugh:

....

Class clown:

....

Most likely to become the president of the USA:

....

Most likely to save an endangered species:

....

Most likely to be a rock star:

....

Most likely to find a cure for the common cold:

....

Here's What I Think About...

....

....

....

....

....

....

....

....

....

....

....

My Crush(es)

Here's how I would describe my attitude about boys:

- ❏ Absolutely boy crazy!
- ❏ Crushing on a couple boys at once
- ❏ Got my eye on one cutie
- ❏ Boys make good friends—that's all
- ❏ I don't understand boys
- ❏ I'm too shy to talk to boys
- ❏ Boys smell funny and are generally gross

My first crush:

I Kaser   crush on kaser:

What I liked about him was...

he's funny smart wierd.

My current crush:

is Kyler

What I like about him is...

funny wierd.cool

My celebrity crush:

....

What I like about him is...

....

My sports crush:

....

What I like about him is...

....

My friends' crushes:

....Cordelia....... likes _Kace_ ....

....Stella........... likes _Roman_ ....

....Elanor......... likes _Adisin_ ....

Of all the boys I know...

............Kyler............... has the best smile.

............Kyler............... has the nicest eyes.

.... is kind to everyone.

............Kyler............... thinks he's the coolest.

.... is fun to talk to.

For I know that nothing can keep us from the love of God.
Romans 8:38

Friends Buds Pals Amigos

....

....

....

_____

....

....

....

....

....

....

Doodle pages

Loving God means to obey His Word, and His Word is not hard to obey
1 John 5:3

....
....
....
....
....
....
....
....
....
....
....
....

Girly Girl Glam Pink Glitter

....

....

....

....

....

....

....

....

....

....

....

....

My Pets

My pets and their names:

....

....

....

....

Best tricks:

....

....

....

....

Birthdays:

....

....

....

....

Favorite treats:

....

....

....

....

Here's how I describe my pets:

☐ Friendly	☐ Smart	☐ Shy
☐ Soft	☐ Cute	☐ Dumb
☐ Warm	☐ Beautiful	☐ Loyal
☐ Snuggly	☐ Handsome	☐ ....
☐ Sassy	☐ Playful	☐ ....
☐ Silly	☐ Hyper	☐ ....

Smile Grin Giggle Wink Laugh

....
....
....
....
....
....
....
....
....
....
....

Give all your worries and cares to God, for he cares about you.
1 Peter 5:7 NLT

....

....

....

....

....

....

....

....

....

....

....

....

My Sports, Clubs, and Hobbies

I am (check all that apply)

- ☐ an actor
- ☑ an artist
- ☐ an athlete
- ☐ a bookworm
- ☐ a crafter
- ☑ a dancer
- ☐ a fashionista

- ☐ a mathlete
- ☑ a musician
- ☐ a scientist
- ☑ a singer
- ☐ a spelling bee champ
- ☑ a writer
- ☐ ....